AXIS PARENT GUIDES SERIES

A PARENT'S GUIDE TO

BODY POSITIVITY

axis

Tyndale House Publishers
Carol Stream, Illinois

Visit Tyndale online at tyndale.com.

Visit Axis online at axis.org.

Tyndale and Tyndale's quill logo are registered trademarks of Tyndale House Ministries.

A Parent's Guide to Body Positivity

For information about special discounts for bulk purchases, please contact Tyndale House Publishers at csresponse@tyndale.com, or call 1-855-277-9400.

Library of Congress Cataloging-in-Publication Data

A catalog record for this book is available from the Library of Congress.

ISBN 978-1-4964-6742-3

Printed in the United States of America

29	28	27	26	25	24	23
7	6	5	4	3	2	1

I could have never imagined how much it would cost me to attempt to reach the standard of today's beauty.

**SADIE ROBERTSON HUFF,
"I WOKE UP LIKE THIS"**

CONTENTS

A LETTER FROM AXIS

Dear Reader,

We're Axis, and since 2007, we've been creating resources to help connect parents, teens, and Jesus in a disconnected world. We're a group of gospel-minded researchers, speakers, and content creators, and we're excited to bring you the best of what we've learned about making meaningful connections with the teens in your life.

This parent's guide is designed to help start a conversation. Our goal is to give you enough knowledge that you're able to ask your teen informed questions about their world. For each guide, we spend weeks reading, researching, and interviewing parents and teens in order to distill everything you need to know about the topic at hand. We encourage you to read the whole thing and then to use the questions we include to get the conversation going with your teen—and then to follow the conversation wherever it leads.

As Douglas Stone, Bruce Patton, and Sheila Heen point out in their book *Difficult Conversations*, "Changes in attitudes and behavior rarely come about because of arguments, facts, and attempts to persuade. How often do *you* change your values and beliefs—or whom you love or what you want in life—based on something someone tells you? And how likely are you to do so when the person who is trying to change you doesn't seem fully aware of the reasons you see things differently in the first place?"[1] For whatever reason, when we believe that others are trying to understand *our* point of view, our defenses usually go down, and we're more willing to listen to *their* point of view. The rising generation is no exception.

So we encourage you to ask questions, to listen, and then to share your heart with your teen. As we often say at Axis, discipleship happens where conversation happens.

Sincerely,
Your friends at Axis

---

[1] Douglas Stone, Bruce Patton, and Sheila Heen, *Difficult Conversations: How to Discuss What Matters Most*, rev. ed. (New York: Penguin Books, 2010), 137.

BEYONCÉ WAS RIGHT: WHEN IT COMES TO BEAUTY, "IT'S THE SOUL THAT NEEDS THE SURGERY"

KATRINA (not her real name) struggled through middle school and high school. It was a difficult time for her—not simply because she was socially awkward, but also because of how she looked. She rarely felt pretty: she struggled on and off with acne, had braces for a while, and had no idea what to do with her crazy hair. To add insult to injury, she didn't know how to dress stylishly and would often feel embarrassed about her clothes.

Our society puts a heavy burden on people—women in particular—to measure up to certain standards of physical beauty. The body positivity movement has arisen in response to these unattainable ideals. It attempts to redefine beauty and human worth and has made its way from social media platforms like Instagram and Twitter into our mainstream marketing. But is it the answer that all teenagers who struggle to accept themselves desperately long for? Despite the necessity of this movement, or at least something like it, body positivity is complicated and nuanced—and very worth talking about with your teens.

The body positivity movement attempts to redefine beauty and human worth and has made its way from social media platforms like Instagram and Twitter into our mainstream marketing.

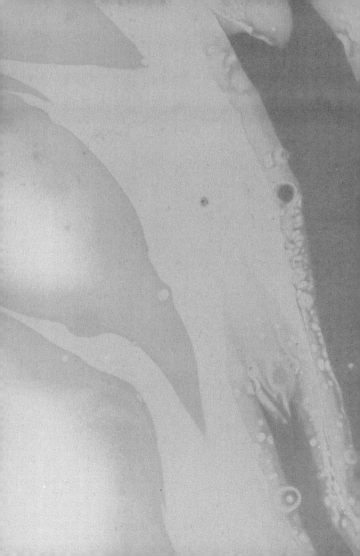

HOW DO TEENS FEEL ABOUT THEIR BODIES?

IN HER BOOK, *Unashamed: Healing Our Brokenness and Finding Freedom from Shame*, Heather Davis Nelson writes, "Shame commonly masquerades as embarrassment, or the nagging sense of 'not quite good enough.'"[1] This is how Katrina felt, and it's a feeling that many teens can relate to, especially when it comes to their bodies. A 2011 study found that 53 percent of thirteen-year-old girls dislike their bodies. By age seventeen, that number increases to 78 percent.[2] The Dove personal care brand says that "the percentage of women who would describe themselves as beautiful is just 4% globally."[3] The creators of the documentary *Straight/Curve* report that 90 percent of women and girls say that media makes them feel worse about how they look and does not accurately represent their body types.[4]

In her TED talk, "Why Thinking You're Ugly Is Bad for You," Dove's Meaghan Ramsey says that 60 percent of girls are making decisions (like choosing whether or not to participate in class discussions) based on whether they think they look good enough.[5] And while men arguably receive less overall negativity about their bodies, they deal with body image issues as well.[6] A study reported by *Time* magazine found that men are almost equally as likely as women to lack confidence about how they look.[7]

SO WHAT IS BODY POSITIVITY?

AT ITS CORE, it's a movement that intends to help people radically accept their and others' bodies just as they are.[8] This acceptance, at least in theory, includes throwing off unrealistic norms surrounding weight, shape, gender, race, age, acne, body hair, cellulite, stretch marks, and even disorders or disabilities. The movement also advocates for more diversity in our mainstream media, rather than a narrow spectrum of people who are considered attractive.

WHO PROMOTES IT?

INSTAGRAM AND TWITTER INFLUENCERS, as well as models making new waves in the industry, are the primary voices of the body positivity movement. Social media stars promoting body positivity include Sonja Renee Taylor (#badpicturemonday), Jessamyn Stanley (yoga star), Megan Jayne Crabbe (anorexia survivor), Virgie Tovar (creator of #losehatenotweight), and Tess Holiday, a plus-size model who created the hashtag #effyourbeautystandards.[9]

Iskra Lawrence is a plus-size model who signed with Aerie, American Eagle's lingerie brand.[10] Since 2014, Aerie has been running a #realbeauty campaign, where it commits not to photoshop any of its models. Ashley Graham is a plus-size model who has been featured multiple times on the cover of *Sports Illustrated*'s swimsuit edition. She also became the first plus-size model to appear on the cover of American *Vogue* in its March 2017 issue.[11]

Unfortunately, but perhaps unsurprisingly, advertisers are also latching on to body positivity as a marketing ploy. Some of the most popular body positivity hashtags are:

- #bodypositivity
- #bodypositive
- #bopo
- #selflove
- #bopofitsall
- #adipositivity
- #fatacceptance
- #plussize
- #plussize fashion
- #plussizeootd

WHY IS THE MOVEMENT GAINING GROUND?

BECAUSE SOMETHING ISN'T WORKING. People are starting to get fed up with the airbrushed "perfection" in images and on our screens. One Dove video (https://www.youtube.com/watch?v=iYhCn0jf46U) illustrates just how much real people can be modified into something completely different from how they actually look.[12] Yet many of us are still living in deep shame over what our bodies look like. In Taryn Brumfitt's documentary *Embrace*, actress and TV personality Ricki Lake says that she can't imagine what it would be like to go through her life not worried about her weight. *[Note: The documentary is on Netflix, and we think it asks good questions about what we assume to be true about beauty and femininity. BUT it is not for undiscerning eyes because it contains quite a bit of nonsexualized female nudity.]*

Amanda de Cadenet, the youngest woman to shoot the cover of *Vogue*, describes how when she was at her thinnest, it was the most miserable time of her life. For her to stay at a size medium, she had to obsess over food and exercise and take her focus off her family. She describes it as "hell on earth." And the airbrushed standard carries over into every physical attribute we have: weight, skin, hair, whether we wear glasses or braces, our facial structure, whether we have a disfigurement, our pores—*anything*.

Just about everyone deals with body shame, even if they meet culture's standards. When you start exploring why people feel shame about their bodies, something that's striking is that anyone can struggle with it, from the models at the top of their industry to people who are severely disfigured. It's remarkable and saddening how skewed people's perceptions of themselves can be. The short film *Dove Real Beauty Sketches* shows a forensic artist sketching women according to their own descriptions of themselves and then sketching them according to other people's descriptions of them. For many of the women, their own perceptions of their appearances were much more negative than how they actually looked.[13]

Body shame starts early in life. Even very young girls experience body shame. A video by *Allure* magazine shows girls between the ages of six and eighteen talking about how they feel about their bodies. It seems that by around age ten, all the girls in the video have started to feel some embarrassment or shame about their bodies, whether because of their own insecurities or because of comments other people have made to them.[14]

It's common for women to depend on makeup to feel okay with how they look. Many women and teen girls would never go out in public without any makeup on. In the video "Women Go without Makeup for a Day," one woman says, "I've been wearing makeup for so long that it's almost become part of my identity."[15] One woman who teaches at a Christian school attempted to do a project with some younger teenage girls, encouraging them to go without makeup for a day. Her goal was to help the girls not to depend on makeup and to value themselves for who God made them to be. She was unprepared for the response she got. The anxiety of the girls was so great and the backlash from their parents so strong that she was unable to move forward with her project.

But this isn't new. The Amazon Prime show *The Marvelous Mrs. Maisel*, set in 1958, depicts a woman who leaves the blinds open just enough that the sun will wake her up in the morning before her husband's alarm goes off. She does this so that she can get up, wash her face, apply her makeup, and fix her hair before she scrambles back into bed in order to look like she woke up like that. She also waits until her husband falls asleep at night before going into the bathroom to remove all her makeup and put her hair in curlers so that he never sees her not all fixed up. (It's later revealed that she learned this tactic from her mother.) Though the show is fiction, it's based on real attitudes from the 1950s and 1960s (especially in upper classes and in certain parts of the US) that women should never be seen not looking their best.

The internet enables us to be more comfortable with hypocrisy and cruelty. In the video "You Look Disgusting," one YouTuber reveals what she looks like both with and without makeup, as well as how people online reacted to her in both cases. What's ironic and upsetting is the fact that people made horrible, hateful comments to her both when she wasn't wearing makeup and when she was. She couldn't win, no matter what she chose to do.[16] Similarly, when actress Mila Kunis lost a lot of weight for a role, her fans accused her of having an eating disorder. Then they turned around and criticized her when she gained the weight back.[17]

Gender dysphoria brings body image issues to a whole new level. People in the LGBTQ+ community often deal with body shame at an entirely different level. Trans people commonly experience gender

One of the challenges that men in particular face is that few people recognize that men even struggle with body image.

dysphoria, meaning they do not feel that their physical bodies correspond to their gender identities.[18] This is discomfort with one's body at its most extreme. In one video, a young trans person says, "Just because my curves make me dysphoric, that doesn't mean they're . . . ugly."[19]

Men rarely have an outlet for talking about body shame. One article notes that teenage boys can struggle with body issues and eating disorders. [20] One of the challenges that men in particular face is that few people recognize that men even struggle with body image. What's more, there is a social stigma against men opening up and acknowledging that body image is a problem for them, so many of them simply deal with their shame alone.[21]

WHERE DOES THE BODY SHAME COME FROM?

A VARIETY OF PLACES. We've already pointed out how harmful the images in media can be and how people can be incredibly cruel, especially online or when they're young. Many of us can trace our body image struggles back to a certain memory or time in our childhood. It could be that our parents criticized us or that their comments about others or themselves shaped our struggles with body image. Even a simple lack of knowledge of how to dress ourselves, do our hair and makeup, etc., can impact whether or not we feel shame about our bodies. And let's not forget that if we're satisfied and happy with our bodies, then companies lose a lot of money because we stop buying their products. So they have a significant interest in keeping us where we are. All of us are tempted to put our identities somewhere other than in God. One way we can do this is idolizing how we look.

People sometimes feel ashamed of their bodies because of sexual abuse or because they have received unwanted sexual advances. In the *Embrace* documentary we mentioned earlier, Amanda de Cadenet says when she hit puberty and started receiving unwanted sexual advances, she stopped eating as much. She wanted to lose weight so she could be less curvy and "hide" from the sexual attention she was getting.

HOW DOES BODY POSITIVITY HELP?

GOD CREATED ALL BODIES, not just the arbitrary "ideal" that our culture praises. It's good that people in our society are speaking out about the fact that all people are valuable, no matter what they look like. Social media, which can be a conduit for so much hatred, can also be a channel for good. Tess Holliday says, "Instagram allows us 'to cultivate our own experiences. . . . Prior to Instagram, you just saw whatever online. Now you can follow people that are into body positivity, feminism, radical body love, artists.'"[22]

She emphasizes the importance of having a supportive community when it comes to accepting your body for what it is. Many women feel that there isn't any kind of representation for their particular issues, so it's good that there are women with different body types represented in the media. Body positivity advocates are at their best when they focus on health and encourage people to be aware of what their bodies need, not what others are saying is important.

ARE THERE ANY NEGATIVES?

DESPITE THE FACT that a change is needed, there are a number of problems with the body positivity movement.

RELATIVISM.

This movement promotes relativism, which is basically the idea that there is no universal truth, and that truth is different for each individual. Body positivity advocates might say that no one has the right to tell them objectively what is good for their bodies, even if that advice is in the interest of their health.

MANY PEOPLE ARE LEFT OUT.

Another glaring issue is that the body positivity movement is supposed to accept people of all body types. What seems to end up happening, however, is that the movement focuses on curvier women, many of whom have beautiful faces and hourglass figures. So while the movement promotes a body type that *is* different from the stick-thin models we're used to seeing, it leaves out many other types of bodies.

It's great (in some ways) that Ashley Graham is being accepted in the industry even though she doesn't look like the traditional model. But she also has a stereotypically beautiful face. What about representation for people who have severe acne[23] or vitiligo[24]? What about burn victims or people who have serious disfigurements? What about people of other races? The modeling industry is still dominated by white women. When we consider the other body image issues people can have, we realize that we have a long way to go in terms of media representation.

THIN SHAMING.

Thinness has been held up so much as an ideal in our culture that some people in the body positivity movement see no problem with shaming women who are thin. Several years ago, pop singer Meghan Trainor released a song called "All about That Bass" *[warning: language]*, which celebrated having a curvier body and appreciating your beauty for what it is. While it was refreshing for someone to present an alternative vision for physical beauty, the song also has several problems. One is that Trainor equates beauty with sexual desirability. Another is that as she validates women with curvier figures, she demeans women who are skinny, calling them "skinny b****es."

When this song came out and one of our Axis traveling teams spoke about it at a high school, our team tried to point

If being body positive
means that someone
could die earlier because
of their obesity or anorexia,
ignoring that reality in
order to be "body positive"
is hurting those people.

out both the good and problematic aspects of this song. After that presentation, several students came up to us and said that they disagreed with what we had said about the thin shaming. In fact, those students wanted us to know that we had probably lost credibility with the rest of the audience because of our position.

REDEFINING "HEALTHY" CAN BE DANGEROUS.

Another hazard of the body positivity movement is that it can normalize unhealthy behaviors and shut down any conversation about what is or isn't healthy.[25] Body positivity advocates emphasize that extra weight is not necessarily unhealthy and thinness is not necessarily healthy. That's a valid point— we shouldn't automatically assume we know how healthy someone is solely based on our impression of their weight.

But if validating all body types leads us to ignore scientific evidence about physical health, that is a problem. If being body positive means that someone could die earlier because of their obesity or anorexia, ignoring that reality in order to be "body positive" is hurting those people. If you search the hashtags #bopo or #bodypositivity on Instagram, you will likely run across images of girls who are anorexic and are promoting their anorexia as a positive quality. We did this ourselves and saw body positive hashtags in images alongside hashtags like #pro-ana, which is short for "pro anorexia." This is a warped and heartbreaking understanding of body positivity.

IT OFTEN PROMOTES SEXUAL OBJECTIFICATION.

Something else you'll notice if you search body positivity hashtags on Instagram (not exactly something we recommend) is that women of all ages are seeking confidence by posting revealing pictures of themselves. To some extent, we can understand why someone would want to do this. It takes a lot of confidence for someone to reveal herself so publicly with all her imperfections, perceived or otherwise. As one parent told us, her teenage daughter defends posting "sensual" pics as "breaking out of her comfort zone."

But there are significant problems with seeking body positivity by posting semi-naked pictures of yourself. We've mentioned that Ashley Graham has been featured on *Sports Illustrated*'s swimsuit edition. While it's great that the magazine is open to a woman with a different body type, those images are still highly sexualized and objectifying. It's hard not to question how much Graham is actually helping women to be more body positive and how much she's reinforcing our culture's message that women are only beautiful when men see them as sexual objects.[26]

THE WHOPPER: IT DOESN'T ACTUALLY ADDRESS THE ROOT PROBLEM.

Simply redefining the standard of beauty to be broader and to include more body types doesn't fix the root problem. In fact, all it does is shift our focus from one standard of beauty to another. What *is* the root problem, then? It's that we believe our worth and identity are intrinsically connected to our outward appearance. And specifically tied to that, we have come to fear people more than we fear and believe God. (More on this below.) Any solution that doesn't address these issues will be, at best, a Band-Aid over a gaping wound.

WHAT'S THE ANSWER?

IN RESPONSE TO SOME of the shortcomings of body positivity, the "body neutrality" movement, which is less about loving oneself and more about learning to not hate oneself, is gaining ground.[27] Autumn Whitefield-Madrano, author of *Face Value: The Hidden Ways Beauty Shapes Women's Lives*, explains:

> My problem with body love, beside the fact that it's a high standard, is it's asking women to regulate their emotions, not just their bodies. I don't see the pressure on women really easing up, and then you're supposed to have this bulletproof self-esteem on top of all that. It's not something we can really live up to. Body love keeps the focus on the body. The times I'm happiest are when I'm not thinking about my body at all.[28]

What a powerful idea that all humans could learn from: perhaps, rather than focusing even more on our bodies, we need to simply deemphasize them so we can devote our thoughts, emotions, and energy to something better.

Body neutrality aims to help people use the mental energy they would've spent thinking about their physical appearance to care about other, more important things. It doesn't encourage forgetting everything and diving headlong into a pile of chips; instead, it promotes learning to listen to our bodies and find the things that truly feel good to each of us (one person may enjoy running while another prefers dancing) while accepting that different periods and phases of life will require different approaches to physical health. For example, there may be a period of six months where a person doesn't get a ton of sleep or have time to cook her own meals because she is hustling to start a business. But after that six-month period, things might slow down, so the person can focus more on having better habits and refueling her body with food and exercise.

While body neutrality addresses a lot of the shortcomings of the body positivity movement, **it still isn't the answer in and of itself**. Why? Because our relationships with our bodies can only be restored to the original flourishing that God intended through the power of Christ. We can do everything that either body positivity or body neutrality asks of us, *but without Christ's power, grace, and redemption, we will never have the right relationship with ourselves and with the bodies he so lovingly crafted.*

Perhaps, rather than focusing even more on our bodies, we need to simply deemphasize them so we can devote our thoughts, emotions, and energy to something better.

WHAT CAN
I DO?

REMEMBER THAT GOD DEFINES OUR WORTH AND BEAUTY.

God has the power to redeem the deepest lies we believe and the brokenness we experience. But we also know that the process of moving from lies to truth is *not* easy. It will probably take some time. It's not easy to believe that we are valuable for who we are when all around us our culture says our worth depends on unattainable standards of physical beauty. But it is *possible* to resist the lies that inundate us and to walk in the freedom that Jesus died to purchase for us.

What does God say about our worth? In Psalm 139:14, David writes, "I will give thanks to You, because I am awesomely and wonderfully *made*; wonderful are Your works, and *my soul knows it very well*" (emphasis added). When God sent the prophet Samuel to anoint the next king after Saul, Samuel thought the king would be one of David's brothers. But God told Samuel, "God does not *see* as man sees, since man looks at the outward appearance, but the LORD looks at the heart."[29] Ephesians 2 reminds us that Jesus died for us even while we were dead in our sins because God is "rich in mercy" and "because of His great love with which He loved us."[30] He loved us when we were unlovable and continues to love us more than we can possibly understand.

In *Unashamed*, Heather Davis Nelson encourages us that the primary way to overcome shame is to pursue Christ. When Adam and Eve were filled with shame because of their sin, God clothed them with the skins of animals. Nelson writes, "Only clothing given by God can do anything about the shame you and I wear as a garment, or the shame that we feel we cannot escape because it perpetually unclothes us."[31]

LIVE IN THE LIGHT OF THAT KNOWLEDGE.

Galatians 5:1 says, "It was for freedom that Christ set us free; therefore keep standing firm and do not be subject again to a yoke of slavery." As one Christian writer puts it, "A fear of man often surrounds our deepest vulnerabilities. Yet our love for God breaks that stronghold. The reason Scripture states numerous times to 'fear God' is because we inherently worship our greatest fear—we are *loyal* to it."[32] So how do we actually walk through life no longer slaves to shame and fear, to what others say about us?

While there is room for us to honestly wrestle before God, at some point we need to choose between the lies we believe and the truth that God offers us. We need to cry out to God when we struggle with believing Him. We need to speak the truth out loud to ourselves and take our thoughts captive.[33] God's Word is our primary weapon in combating the lies that dominate us, so we should be proactive in memorizing Scripture and reminding ourselves of what God says.

Heather Davis Nelson recommends that we work on overcoming our shame by figuring out how it started developing in our lives: "Explore what type(s) of shame you typically experience, and chart its development in your story." Then we will be able to "rewrite our shame stories moment by moment," speaking the truth to ourselves about the lies we believe. We need to repent of our idolatry, and we need other people to remind us of the truth and to pray for us. In turn, we ourselves need to empathize with, serve, and encourage one another. Nelson notes that living a shame-free life will take time. It will be difficult at first, but just as physical exercise becomes easier with practice, so living a shame-free life will become second nature to us.[34]

However, some of the lies we believe are deep and complicated and might require professional counseling to fully work through. Don't be afraid or ashamed of seeking out counseling in order to find healing if that's what you and/or your kids need.

RECOGNIZE THAT CULTURAL "STANDARDS" ARE CULTURAL.

Beauty standards have changed over time, and they differ from culture to culture throughout the world. In one video, a woman was Photoshopped to meet the beauty ideals of different countries around the world. The differences are striking.[35]

We have a Chinese friend who worries that being in the sun will make her skin darker. She wants to be as pale as possible. This is the opposite goal of most Americans, who want to be as tan as possible. Neither of these desires is right or wrong; they're just different. Recognizing that beauty standards are subjective won't remove us from the pressure of the culture we live in. But doing so can help us remember that the ideals of our own culture are not universal or absolute.

REMEMBER THAT THE OPPOSITE SEX ISN'T AS CRITICAL OF US AS WE ARE OF OURSELVES.

Don't get us wrong—we are NOT saying that we should find our self-worth in whether or not the opposite sex finds us

attractive. But because the media constantly gives us a narrow vision of beauty,
it can be helpful to hear that guys are
attracted to a variety of qualities, physical and nonphysical, not just stick-thin
model types.[36] And as this article on
male body shame points out, someone
with good character who is looking for a
partner who has good character will not
be overly focused on the physical: "The
twenty things you see in the mirror that
you hate yourself for, they will not regis-
ter for a worthwhile woman."[37]

HOW CAN I HELP MY KIDS HAVE HEALTHY VIEWS OF THEIR BODIES?

FATHERS

Dads, **your daughters need to hear that you think they're beautiful**. As the first and most important man in your daughter's life, you will help shape her vision of how men relate to her. One woman who grew up with two brothers says that her dad never told her she was beautiful. He basically related to her as though she were a guy. As a result, she never believed that other men would find her beautiful. Another woman emphasizes the importance of dads telling their daughters they are beautiful even when the daughters are not dressed up. Your girls need to know you value their character much more than their appearance.

MOTHERS

Moms, nothing will influence your daughters more than you modeling what it looks like to be at peace with your appearance. Your girls need you to guard yourself from projecting your own body image issues on them. In the "Dove Selfie" video on redefining beauty, one high school girl observes that her mom's insecurities affect how the teen sees herself: "When you hear her talk about her insecurities, you start to focus on your own."[38] So if that's where you need to start, we highly recommend doing so and inviting your daughters into the process. Your vulnerability, as difficult and painful as it might be, will encourage them to also be vulnerable and do the necessary work.

Moms, you need to affirm your daughters' value and beauty. Never assume that if your girls have a "more acceptable" body type, they don't need to hear your love and affirmation. It can be beneficial to your daughters if you come alongside them and help them learn how to be good stewards of their bodies. **We say this cautiously with the caveat to be careful with how you communicate.** Offhand comments about your daughters' weight or appearance can be extremely harmful. We know of one woman who is still dealing with the consequences of her mother's remarks when she was a teen. For example, whenever the daughter would eat a dessert, her mother would suggest she go on a run to work off the extra calories. The mother's focus on the daughter's weight and body image damaged this woman's view of herself.

On the other hand, we know a different woman who had bad acne in high school and college and who had tried different products for years with no success. After she gave up on finding anything that would work, her mother continued looking for her and found a product that finally

Dads, your daughters need to hear that you think they're beautiful.

Moms, nothing will
influence your daughters
more than you modeling
what it looks like to
be at peace with your
appearance.

cleared up the acne on her daughter's face. While she knows that her worth isn't based on her appearance, this woman is extremely grateful that her mother shared her burden and didn't give up.

BOTH PARENTS TOGETHER

Everyone feels hopeless about their appearance sometimes. We look in the mirror and see things we have no power to change—things like skin type, nose shape, height, build, hair type, skin color, etc. So while we help our kids unravel the lies about their unchangeable character-istics, it may also be helpful to empower them to change what they can. We can help them see that some goals are achievable. They *can* get in better shape or get stronger or have better hygiene or increase their stamina or whatever their goal is. But let's join them as they endeavor to make those changes, as well as help them find healthy solutions (weight lifting, finding a new sport, mindful eating, and being active outside are much better than endless diets, chronic cardio, or fitness activities they don't enjoy). Help them appreciate hard work and what their bodies can accomplish.

Let's also be thankful for and good stewards of what God has given us! We are not to live our lives based on what culture thinks about us, what other people think about us, or what *we think* other people think about us. We are to live life based on what God thinks about us—and He loves us and finds us immeasurably valuable. People who live in freedom and gratitude will treat their bodies well. It's good and right not only to be thankful for our bodies as they are, but also to take care of them because they are one of God's gifts to us.[39]

WHAT ABOUT MODESTY?

MODESTY DEFINITELY FITS into the body positivity conversation, but we need to rethink it before we talk about it. The church has a history of shaming women of all ages for how they act and dress, often blaming women for men's lust. Though we don't have the room to fully discuss it here, suffice it to say that modesty (defined as "behavior, manner, or appearance intended to avoid impropriety or indecency") is something that should apply to both genders and to all areas of our lives, not just how we dress.

When it comes to accepting our bodies for what they are, it's important to talk to both our sons and our daughters about how posting sexy photos or wearing revealing clothing actually *exacerbates* our insecurities, often driving us to seek for more and more approval of our appearance. In fact, this kind of behavior can make us dislike our bodies even more because we're constantly taking photos of ourselves and looking at what's not "perfect." But instead of just spoon-feeding them the answer (like "dress to honor God and have compassion on those around us"), let's ask questions that get our kids thinking about how best to live in this area. Are there certain rules they should follow? Or is there an underlying principle to apply? How can we tell if we're seeking approval and acceptance in the wrong places? How can we tell if we're seeking them in the right place?

It's important to talk to both our sons and our daughters about how posting sexy photos or wearing revealing clothing actually exacerbates our insecurities, often driving us to seek for more and more approval of our appearance.

SHOULD WE EVER TALK ABOUT PHYSICAL QUALITIES?

IF OUR BODIES DIDN'T MATTER, God wouldn't have given us bodies. But He did. And He also gave us the ability to appreciate them. So we need to be careful not to ignore our bodies or our desire to look and feel good. But we also need to change the way we talk about our own and others' bodies. We often say things like "You look beautiful!" "He's the most attractive man in the world." "If only I could have a body like that." "If only he would take care of himself, he could be decent looking!" and "She let herself go." (Ask your kids if there are things they hear others say about appearance.) Let's briefly discuss each of these statements.

"You look beautiful!" Even though we may be well intentioned, telling someone they *look* beautiful is very different than telling someone they *are* beautiful. It's affirming solely their outward appearance, rather than of who they are, inside and out.

"He's the most attractive man in the world." We are *so quick* to compare one person's appearance to another's. Yes, God made us to be attracted to each other and to have sexual desire, but comparing our attractiveness is not what God intended. **One person's attractiveness does not somehow diminish another person's.** And we are not in competition with one another for the title of "sexiest man/woman alive," no matter what society says.

"If only I could have a body like that." Why? What lies are we believing if we think that looking like someone else will somehow fix our problems? In fact, stereotypically attractive people have just as many insecurities as stereotypically unattractive people, and life doesn't somehow get easier if we are considered attractive. We all still face the same responsibilities and struggles.

"If only he would take care of himself, he could be decent looking!" and **"She let herself go."** Should being attractive be our only reason for taking care of ourselves? And are we really in a position to judge whether someone "let themselves go"? Or is it possible that they're going through something difficult and need help? With statements like these, we judge others, their values, and their circumstances unnecessarily. These comments teach us and our kids that it's okay to judge not only how others look, but also *why* they look that way.

Clearly, our words can be hurtful even when we don't intend for them to be.

Stereotypically attractive people have just as many insecurities as stereotypically unattractive people, and life doesn't somehow get easier if we are considered attractive.

We need to be cognizant of the people around us and speak with compassion at all times. And if we want to encourage our kids (or ourselves!) to value physical health, there are constructive ways of doing so. Some things that might be more helpful to say are:

- "You're beautiful/handsome!"

- "He's so attractive *to me* because [list both physical qualities and character traits you appreciate]."

- "I want to emulate her [dedication to fitness or perseverance or other quality you'd like to learn]."

- "I want to [insert activity goal here, such as work out four times a week or hike a certain mountain]." (This is instead of "I need to lose twenty pounds.")

- "She looks different lately. I wonder if she's going through something. I should catch up with her and make sure everything's okay."

What else can you and your kids come up with as constructive ways of talking about others and about physical health?

RECAP

- Very few women regard themselves as beautiful, and this feeling of not being good enough is picked up during adolescence. Ninety percent of women and girls say that media makes them feel worse about themselves.

- Body positivity is a movement that seeks to combat this issue by helping women learn to love their bodies, flaws and all, and by including more diversity in media.

- Body shame comes from a variety of places, and everyone struggles with it, including those who fit culture's narrow standards of attractiveness.

- While body positivity is great in a lot of ways, it still has many downsides. For instance, it leaves many people out and doesn't actually address the root problem.

- Body neutrality could help because it's less about loving oneself and more about learning not to hate oneself, while also trying to take the focus off the body altogether.

- Without Christ's power, grace, and redemption, we will never have the right relationship with ourselves and the bodies He so lovingly crafted.

- Parents can do a lot to shape their kids' view of themselves, but they must also model this by working on their own relationship with their bodies.

- Our bodies *do* matter, so it's not wrong to notice them. But we need to change how we talk about them.

Parents can do a lot to shape their kids' view of themselves, but they must also model this by working on their own relationship with their bodies.

DISCUSSION QUESTIONS

1. How do you feel about the way you look? Do you mainly enjoy what you look like, or are you ashamed of your appearance? Why do you think that is?

2. What do you enjoy most about how you look?

3. How does our culture influence how you feel about how you look?

4. How do other people influence how you feel about your body?

5. When did you first start feeling embarrassed about some aspect of your appearance?

6. As you go through each day, do you have a particular narrative in your mind telling you what people think about your appearance?

7. What does God think about your beauty and your worth? What are

some verses you can write down and
read as reminders each day?

8. Is there any way that we as
   your parents have encouraged
   or discouraged you about your
   appearance? How can we be more
   encouraging to you in the future?

9. What are some practical ways you
   can encourage or avoid discouraging
   the people around you when it
   comes to their appearances?

10. What are some things that you are
    grateful your body can do? Is there
    a way to better learn or appreciate
    what your body's capable of?

11. Is there one aspect of your health
    you'd like to work on? How can we
    help you with that?

CONCLUSION

AUTHOR AND SPEAKER Sadie Robertson Huff points out, "If who you are now is not enough for you, then it will never be enough until your perspective changes and your heart takes a shift."[40] Your kids need to know that their value, worth, and beauty come from being made in the image and by the hand of an infinitely loving God—not from anything or anyone else. They need you to walk in the light of that freedom so you can mentor them as well. With your help, they can go through life confident in who they are in Christ, instead of living in the shame that comes from a false reality. And even though most adults know that truly accepting oneself can be a lifelong journey, we parents have the ability to start our kids down the path to true freedom and flourishing now, rather than after years of pain and suffering.

ADDITIONAL RESOURCES

1. More Than a Body, https://www.more thanabody.org

2. "Body Positivity or Body Obsession? Learning to See More & Be More," TEDx Talk by Lindsay Kite, https://www.you tube.com/watch?v=uDowwh0EU4w&t=11s

3. "From Body Hatred to Believing I'm Beautiful: My Radical Change of Clothes," Boundless, https://www.boundless.org /blog/body-hated-believing-im-beautiful -radical-change-clothes/

4. "Dove Inner Critic," https://www.dove .com/us/en/stories/campaigns/inner -critic.html

5. "Sam Claflin on Why He's Speaking Out against Male Body Shaming," E! News, https://www.eonline.com/news/859607 /sam-claflin-on-why-he-s-speaking-out -against-male-body-shaming

6. "Sam Smith and 9 Other Male Celebs on Body Image," BBC, https://www.bbc.com /news/entertainment-arts-40863606

7. "Fans Are Pissed That This Body-Positive Instagram Star Had Skin Removal Surgery,"

Buzzfeed, https://www.buzzfeed.com
/morganshanahan/this-body-positive
-instagrammer-is-being-body-shamed-for

8. "When Body Positivity Gets Ugly," Viva,
https://vocal.media/viva/when-body
-positivity-gets-ugly

9. "Women Get Photoshopped into Cultural
Beauty Standards" (*warning: strong
language*), https://www.youtube.com
/watch?v=WwLGb5RDcG0%20%27

NOTES

1. Heather Davis Nelson, *Unashamed: Healing Our Brokenness and Finding Freedom from Shame* (Wheaton, IL: Crossway, 2016), 17.

2. Cameron Russell, "Looks Aren't Everything. Believe Me, I'm a Model," TED Talk, YouTube, video, 9:37, January 16, 2013, https://www.youtube.com/watch?v=KM4Xe6DlpOY.

3. "Dove Ad Makeover," Dove, accessed May 31, 2022, https://www.dove.com/us/en/stories/campaigns/ad-makeover.html.

4. *Straight/Curve: Redefining Body Image*, video, 2:06, http://www.straightcurvefilm.com/.

5. Meaghan Ramsey, "Why Thinking You're Ugly Is Bad for You," TED Talk, YouTube, video, 12:06, May 5, 2017, https://www.youtube.com/watch?v=MyUreckKJ1Y.

6. Sile Walsh, "What Men Hate about Their Bodies (and How to Help Them Love Themselves Again)," The Good Men Project, October 25, 2015, https://goodmenproject

.com/featured-content/what-men-hate
-about-their-bodies-and-how-to-help-them
-love-themselves-again-dg/.

7. Megan Lasher, "Men and Women Are Equally
Unhappy with How They Look, Study Says,"
Time, May 31, 2016, https://time.com/4352400
/men-women-body-image/.

8. "What Is the Body Positivity Movement?"
Bustle, YouTube, video, 4:09, November 18,
2015, https://www.youtube.com/watch?v
=6tTmYmc6ubE.

9. Maya Salam, "Why 'Radical Body Love' Is
Thriving on Instagram," *New York Times*, June
9, 2017, https://www.nytimes.com/2017/06/09
/style/body-positive-instagram.html.

10. Ariana Marsh, "Aerie Releases New
Unretouched Campaign," *Teen Vogue*, January
25, 2018, https://www.teenvogue.com/story
/aerie-releases-new-unretouched-campaign.

11. Sophia Chabbott, "Ashley Graham Becomes
First 'Plus-Size' Model to Grace *Vogue* Cover,"
Women's Wear Daily, February 9, 2017, https://
wwd.com/business-news/media/vogue

-features-first-plus-size-model-ashley
-graham-on-march-2017-cover-10781777/.

12. "Dove Evolution," YouTube, video, 1:14,
October 6, 2006, https://www.youtube.com
/watch?v=iYhCn0jf46U.

13. "Dove Real Beauty Sketches | You're More
Beautiful Than You Think," Dove US, YouTube,
video, 3:00, April 14, 2013, https://www.youtube
.com/watch?v=XpaOjMXyJGk.

14. "Girls Ages 6–18 Talk about Body Image,"*Allure*,
YouTube, video, 5:44, May 31, 2018, https://
www.youtube.com/watch?v=5mP5RveA_tk.

15. "Women Go Without Makeup for a Day," As/
Is, YouTube, video, 5:11, April 30, 2017, https://
www.youtube.com/watch?v=muClTcWnH1c.

16. "You Look Disgusting," My Pale Skin, YouTube,
video, 3:11, July 1, 2015, https://www.youtube
.com/watch?v=WWTRwj9t-vU.

17. "10 Celebs Who Gained Weight and LOVED
IT," TheThings Celebrity, YouTube, video,
10:50, June 7, 2018, https://www.youtube
.com/watch?v=TBdWcaVYFJU.

18. "What Is Gender Dysphoria?," American Psychiatric Association, November 2020, https://www.psychiatry.org/patients-families /gender-dysphoria/what-is-gender-dysphoria.

19. "Trans Body Positivity," ChandlerNWilson, YouTube, video, 12:32, January 22, 2017, https://www.youtube.com/watch?v =MUJPYFbIKDM.

20. Anonymous, "Body Issues Affect Our Boys, Too," Momtastic, accessed May 31, 2022, https://www.momtastic.com/parenting /773733-body-issues-affect-our-boys-too/.

21. Tyler Kingkade, "I'm a Man with Body Image Issues, and Now I Know I'm Not Alone," *HuffPost*, August 20, 2015, https://www .huffpost.com/entry/male-body-image -problems_n_55d538fde4b07addcb458638.

22. Salam, "Why 'Radical Body Love' Is Thriving on Instagram."

23. "Is Acne the Final Frontier of Body Positivity? | i-D," YouTube, video, 3:25, June 15, 2018, https://www.youtube.com/watch?v =HTZoNGJyj7o.

24. "Vitiligo," Wikipedia, accessed May 31, 2022, https://en.wikipedia.org/wiki/Vitiligo.

25. University of East Anglia, "Normalization of 'Plus-Size' Risks Hidden Danger of Obesity, Study Finds," EurekAlert!, June 22, 2018, https://www.eurekalert.org/news-releases /531340.

26. Jessica Cwynar-Horta, "The Commodification of the Body Positive Movement on Instagram," *Stream: Culture/Politics/Technology* 8, no. 2 (2016): 36–56, https://journals.sfu.ca/stream /index.php/stream/article/view/203/180.

27. Anna Kessel, "The Rise of the Body Neutrality Movement: 'If You're Fat, You Don't Have to Hate Yourself,'" *Guardian*, July 23, 2018, https://www.theguardian.com/lifeandstyle /2018/jul/23/the-rise-of-the-body-neutrality -movement-if-youre-fat-you-dont-have-to -hate-yourself.

28. Marisa Meltzer, "Forget Body Positivity: How About Body Neutrality?," The Cut, March 1, 2017, https://www.thecut.com/2017/03/forget -body-positivity-how-about-body-neutrality .html.

29. 1 Samuel 16:7

30. See Ephesians 2:4.

31. Nelson, *Unashamed*, 28.

32. Eric Demeter, "Freedom from Shame, Strength in Vulnerability," Boundless, August 4, 2014, https://www.boundless.org/faith/freedom -from-shame-strength-in-vulnerability/.

33. See 2 Corinthians 10:5.

34. Nelson, *Unashamed*, 108.

35. "Beauty Standards around the World," As/Is, YouTube, video, 2:05, June 28, 2014, https:// www.youtube.com/watch?v=RT9FmDBrewA.

36. Ross Boone, "The Finding Flaw," Boundless, February 16, 2017, https://www.boundless.org /blog/the-finding-flaw/.

37. "The Epidemic of Male Body Hatred," The Best Male, September 10, 2019, https://thebestmale .com/the-epidemic-of-male-body-hatred/.

38. "Dove Selfie | Redefining Beauty One Photo at a Time," Dove US, YouTube, video, 8:03, January 19, 2014, https://www.youtube.com /watch?v=BFkm1Hg4dTI.

39. Elise Bryant, "Your Body Is a Temple," Boundless, May 11, 2020, https://www .boundless.org/blog/your-body-is-a-temple/.

40. Sadie Robertson Huff, "I Woke Up Like This," Live Original, September 1, 2017, https:// liveoriginal.com/2017-sadie-robertson-i -woke-up-like-this/.

PARENT GUIDES TO SOCIAL MEDIA
BY AXIS

It's common to feel lost in your teen's world. Let these be your go-to guides on social media, how it affects your teen, and how to begin an ongoing conversation about faith that matters.

BUNDLE THESE 5 BOOKS AND SAVE

DISCOVER MORE PARENT GUIDES, VIDEOS, AND AUDIOS AT AXIS.ORG

PARENT GUIDES TO FINDING TRUE IDENTITY
BY AXIS

When culture is constantly pulling teens away from Christian values, let these five parent guides spark an ongoing conversation about finding your true identity in Christ.

BUNDLE THESE 5
BOOKS AND SAVE